JUS†ICE
FOR THE UNREACHED

JUSTICE

FOR THE UNREACHED

NICK ROBERTSON

MORNING JOY MEDIA
POTTSTOWN, PENNSYLVANIA

Published by Morning Joy Media.

Visit morningjoymedia.com for more information on bulk discounts and special promotions, or email your questions to info@morningjoymedia.com.

Cover Design: Eliana Soares

BISAC Subject Headings:

RELIGION / Christian Ministry / Evangelism
RELIGION / Christian Living / Social Issues

ISBN 978-1-937107-79-6 (paperback)

ISBN 978-1-937107-80-2 (ebook)

Printed in the United States of America

This book is dedicated to my daughters. I am grateful for you, your love, and your patience with me as we serve together among the unreached.

Thanks also to my wife for her editing and encouragement throughout this project. I love you!

CONTENTS

PREFACE

2025

Justice for the Unreached was published in 2014, over ten years ago. Since then, the number of people unreached with the good news has grown from two billion to over three billion. While the body of Christ has done much to spread the good news to those without access to Christ, our task has grown even more. There is still a huge need to focus on the unreached.

Along with some changing population statistics, Western culture has continued growing more secular. This secularism has affected the church in many ways. Society continues to focus on the material, denying the transcendent. More and more laws ignore God's standards of justice and instead focus on whatever seems to promote secular ideals.

The gist of the stories told in the 2014 edition are kept in the same format. Keep that in mind when specific ages and timelines are mentioned. Though these stories are not as new as when told in 2014, they are still accurate and highlight the spiritual points they are meant to illustrate.

THE SIGNIFICANCE OF JUSTICE

Why does justice matter?

P overty, slavery, food insecurity, lack of clean drinking
water, homelessness, trafficking, racism, illiteracy. These
causes have grabbed people's attention worldwide, and right-
fully so! It should bother us to know that people do not have
sufficient food to eat. It should disturb us that slavery still exists
in our world. We should be alarmed that people still face dis-
crimination because of their skin color and ethnic background.
Justice should matter deeply to each of us.

The theme of justice has particularly taken hold of the
hearts of Western teens and young adults. Rallying for causes
has never been more popular in the world than it is today.
Today's youth are often riveted to social justice causes.

Justice Reflects God's Heart

Even more important than contemporary interest in justice
is God's heart. Justice matters greatly to God! It is not God's
plan for children to go to bed hungry. It is not His design for
women to be abused and used by society. God does not desire
for people to be unable to read or to live in poverty. God never
intended for people to become sick from drinking impure
water or to die from AIDS. God created this world and its

people to live in beauty, love, joy, and peace. Sin destroyed His creation—and God longs to restore our broken world to its original glory! Justice reflects God's heart.

Justice Reflects God's Character

Justice is also important because justice reflects God's character. It is who He is. God Himself is just. We read in the Bible over and over that God loves justice.

- The LORD has made himself known; he has executed judgment. (Psalm 9:16)

- The LORD works righteousness and justice for all who are oppressed. (Psalm 103:6)

- I know that the LORD will maintain the cause of the afflicted and will execute justice for the needy. (Psalm 140:12)

Justice is part of God's nature. As we grow in our knowledge and understanding of God, we will naturally grow in our understanding of and love for justice. Loving God leads us to love justice.

Justice Is Expected from Believers

Justice should matter to Christ-followers because justice matters to our God. Justice is the expected behavior of those who follow God. When answering the question, "And what does the LORD require of you?" the prophet Micah's first response is "But to do justice" (Micah 6:8). God loves justice, and He requires His followers to love justice as well.

* Keep justice, and do righteousness, for soon my salvation will come, and my righteousness be revealed. (Isaiah 56:1)

* Blessed are they who observe justice, who do righteousness at all times. (Psalm 106:3)

God expects us to treat others justly. Jesus even defined the second greatest commandment as loving our neighbor as ourselves.[1] How can we possibly love our neighbor to that degree without being concerned they experience justice? There is no way to truly love fellow human beings without desiring them to receive justice in their circumstances and life. As we seek to follow Christ's command to love, justice should mark all of our actions. Believers should be known as agents and promoters of justice.

Justice Benefits Society

Justice is also essential for the well-being of nations. Countries cannot flourish if justice is constantly perverted. Justice helps provide needed stability.

* By justice a king builds up the land, but one who exacts gifts tears it down. (Proverbs 29:4)

* You shall not pervert justice. You shall not show partiality, and you shall not accept a bribe, for a bribe blinds the eyes of the wise and subverts the cause of the righteous. (Deuteronomy 16:19)

* You shall do no injustice in court. You shall not be partial to the poor or defer to the great, but in righteousness you shall judge your neighbor. (Leviticus 19:15)

Corruption, deceit, revolutions, looting, violence, and war typify geographical areas that lack justice. When justice is absent, citizens live in fear and anxiety. The presence of justice, on the other hand, creates an atmosphere of trust, hope, and opportunity. Nations can grow and develop when justice is practiced.

Join the Conversation

1. Why is justice important? Give biblical and personal reasons.

2. How do you promote justice in your daily life?

3. Which of the Bible verses in this chapter impacted you the most? How?

2

WHOLISTIC JUSTICE

For what will it profit a man if he gains the whole world and forfeits his soul? [2]

J ustice has both *physical* and *spiritual* dimensions. God desires justice to be demonstrated in both domains. In His inaugural address in His home synagogue, Jesus, reading from Isaiah, proclaimed:

> The Spirit of the Lord is upon me, because he has anointed me to proclaim good news to the poor. He has sent me to proclaim liberty to the captives and recovering of sight to the blind, to set at liberty those who are oppressed, to proclaim the year of the Lord's favor. [3]

Jesus' heart for physical or material justice rings true and clear in His recitation of Isaiah. He demonstrated a heart for people experiencing poverty and those in prison. He also acknowledged the importance of physical healing.

However, we would be remiss if we stopped at a simple materialistic interpretation of Jesus' words. The deeper meaning of Jesus' words points to alleviating physical *and spiritual* suffering. Setting captives free is even more of a spiritual exercise than a physical one.

Experiencing true liberty is also much more than being set free from a physical jail or the chains of slavery. True liberty is the product of spiritual freedom that only Christ can give. Recovery of physical sight is impressive, but opening spiritually blind eyes can be more difficult. It certainly has more long-term ramifications.

> Jesus' use of the verbs *preach* and *proclaim* emphasizes the importance of spiritual justice, which comes through encounters with God's truth.

Jesus' use of the verbs *preach* and *proclaim* emphasizes the importance of spiritual justice, which comes through encounters with God's truth. When we proclaim God's truth, people have the opportunity to receive freedom from the bondage caused by satanic lies. People who know the truth have the choice to be set free! Yes, physical acts meeting material needs are necessary, but we must never forget the impact of spoken spiritual acts, which allow eternal breakthroughs.

The Priority of Spiritual Justice

As Christ-followers, we should be concerned about physical justice while prioritizing the great need for spiritual justice. Jesus modeled this in Mark 2 when some friends brought their paralyzed friend to him for physical healing. The friends even made a hole in the roof above where Jesus was teaching to enable them to help their friend access Jesus. Jesus' initial concern, however, was not for the man's physical condition.

Mark 2:5 says, "And when Jesus saw their faith, he said to the paralytic, 'Son, your sins are forgiven.'"

Most likely, the friends' aim in lowering the man who was paralyzed through the roof was *not* to help him get forgiveness for his sin. Their main aim was probably physical healing. Jesus, though, emphasized the *priority* of the spiritual over the natural by first saying, "Son, your sins are forgiven."

While we should never diminish the importance of addressing physical needs, meeting spiritual needs is even more critical. Jesus demonstrated the priority of spiritual needs, even over meeting the needs of a paralyzed man. Jesus did heal the paralysis as well, but in the process, Jesus demonstrated His authority to forgive sins, a spiritual need.

Spiritual justice is even more critical than physical justice for at least two reasons:

First, the spiritual world is even more real than the physical world.

Hebrews 11:3 reminds us that the spiritual world existed before the physical world. "What is seen was not made out of things that are visible." The physical world came into existence through God, who is spirit.[4]

Setting someone free from spiritual bondages and addictions is even more critical than setting someone free from a physical jail. Throughout the Bible, God's people have been spiritually free when imprisoned. Paul and Silas were spiritually free in Acts 16 as they sang songs of praise to God at midnight. Peter was spiritually free when the church prayed for his freedom in Acts 12. On the other hand, many people who are apart from Christ are not physically imprisoned but rather bound by addictions, lusts, and life-controlling habits.

Second, spiritual justice is more important than physical justice because the spiritual world lasts forever.

Paul writes, "As we look not to the things that are seen but to the things that are unseen. For the things that are seen are transient, but the things that are unseen are eternal."[5] Our life in the spiritual world lasts forever, and eternal separation from God—eternal suffering—is even worse than any suffering on earth.

As Christ-followers, we must prioritize spiritual justice while not neglecting physical justice. John Piper remarked about this during a plenary session in Lausanne III (a famous missions conference) in Cape Town. He asked, "Could Lausanne say? Could the Evangelical Church say, 'For Christ's sake, we Christians care about all suffering, especially eternal suffering'?"[6]

Emphasizing Wholistic Justice

Jesus is concerned about physical needs. While on earth, Jesus healed everyone who came to him to be healed. No one left disappointed. Jesus also fed large crowds of people on at least two occasions.[7]

Jesus also understood the great importance of spiritual needs. While caring for people's physical needs, He emphasized the great importance of their relationship with God. Jesus cared about temporal *and* eternal suffering.

David Leatherberry served people experiencing poverty in Afghanistan for many years by distributing food and milk. He recognized the importance of the Afghans receiving physical food, but he also discerned their desperate need for spiritual truth. David writes:

If I lift the Afghan out of his poverty and do not proclaim Christ by my life and words, I do not love him. If, in reality, my first concern is relieving his physical suffering and not the eternal destiny of his soul, I do not love him. If I am only the hands and feet of Jesus and not his mouth also, I pervert the gospel and fail Christ.[8]

We must present the wholistic gospel, which recognizes the priority of our spiritual lives while not ignoring physical needs. Often, others are more open to receiving physical aid than spiritual aid. We, as Christians, frequently get more recognition for supplying physical aid than spiritual aid to others, but we must remember the great importance of spiritual justice. We must not neglect to share God's eternal truth because meeting physical needs is more culturally rewarding.

Finally, as we consider the great importance of spiritual justice, we must remember the question Jesus asked,

"What will it profit a man if he *gains the whole world* and *forfeits his soul?*"[9]

In a similar manner we should ask,

What will it profit someone if they gain food on earth yet live in spiritual (and physical) hunger *forever and ever?*

What will it profit someone to get new clothes on earth yet be *eternally* clothed in the shame of sin?

What will it profit someone to gain even freedom from trafficking here on earth yet live in *eternal* bondage?

Today's cultural, political, and even religious environments often emphasize seeking justice only for physical needs. As Christ-followers, we must seek wholistic justice, which addresses both physical and spiritual needs. As Christ-followers, we must especially seek justice that lasts forever.

Join the Conversation

1. How does Jesus' quoting Isaiah 61 in Luke 4 refer to both spiritual and physical justice?

2. Why do so many conversations about justice focus only on physical needs?

3. What are two reasons spiritual justice is even more important than physical justice?

3

JESUS: ESSENTIAL FOR JUSTICE

Can true justice exist without Jesus?

The injustices of poverty, racism, food insecurity, trafficking, lack of clean drinking water, and illiteracy are all social justice issues that get much attention in Western cultures. These issues all reveal the reality of a broken world. They point to crises that noble people with good intentions attempt to fix. The trouble is this: These issues can only be fully resolved by bringing Jesus Christ into the picture.

Believers must be concerned with the root issues that only Jesus can address. Giving money to people experiencing poverty can be good, but giving money does not address the root issues causing poverty. Only Jesus can provide true dignity and break off poverty's spiritual and physical aspects. Helping to alleviate physical suffering due to AIDS and trafficking is essential, but root issues must be addressed to bring long-term change in communities. People need Jesus to be truly freed from the shame, depression, lust, and greed that accompany sexual sin and abuse. If we want to erase social injustice from society, we *must* introduce Jesus. Jesus is essential for *true* justice.

God Alone Defines True Justice

Part of the challenge with justice is establishing how it is determined. By what standard is something unjust? Our human perspective is extremely limited. It is so easy to make an assumption based on wrong or partial information and then to make a judgment based on our assumption of what was fair, only to discover we lacked critical information. Another trap is judging what is fair by comparing our experience with someone else's. Furthermore, what we feel is fair and what our neighbor feels is fair may be completely different. Nations may not agree with other nations regarding what is just and what is not.

How is justice defined when so many opinions and view-points exist? We need God's revelation to make the right judgments about justice. Only God is all-knowing and all-wise. He sees everything, and He alone determines true justice. Only God defines the standard of true justice.

Jesus Recognizes a Person's True Value

The value a society ascribes to individuals affects the rights, privileges, and protections its citizens enjoy. Many societies are based primarily on worldviews that do not acknowledge the intrinsic value of each individual. Some belief systems in Asia, for instance, see animals as having value equal to humans. In some societies, there are harsher consequences for harming an animal than a human being. Other societies value individuals based on their gender. Western societies often ascribe value based on physical appearance, bank account, athletic prowess, or fame. These warped worldviews devalue people and promote injustice.

Rekha lives in South Asia with her three daughters. All three girls, ages 11, 9, and 8, are severely developmentally challenged. None of them can speak. The society in which they live has assigned a value to their lives, and that value is little to nothing. Not only are they girls, they are mentally challenged. They have never had the opportunity to go to school. They are regularly hit and beaten. Local villagers call them crazy.

While Rekha's community does not value her or her girls, Jesus does. He proved their value when He gave His life for them on a cross. Jesus does not assign value to Rekha's girls based on their gender or mental ability. Instead, He sees them for who they are: girls made in His image.

Furthermore, Jesus, who taught us to love our neighbors as ourselves, alone can enable us to love people truly and demonstrate true justice. His love alone is genuine and without prejudice. Humans inherently have all sorts of prejudices that can easily distort justice. Even in the West, where tolerance is viewed as the greatest of virtues and racism is viewed as the greatest of sins, prejudice still abounds. Bias for one's race, community, or ethnic group continues. Only Christ can enable people to live without any prejudice.

Eliminating the Roots of Injustice

Only Jesus can deliver from the root causes of injustice: sin and satan. Sin separates us from God and causes people to fall short of the potential God created them to have.[10] Sin severely mars our ability to be just or promote justice. Only Jesus can set us free from sin and give us new life![11]

Jesus also gives us the ability to overcome satan, who promotes injustice however he can, always seeking to kill, steal, and destroy.[12] Jesus came to destroy satan's works.[13] Jesus came to preach good news to the poor[14] and taught us to love our neighbor as ourselves.[15]

Seeking justice without Jesus is like putting a bandage on a mortal wound. We may slow the blood loss, but death is still going to result. Some temporal relief for the victim and assuagement of guilt for ourselves occurs when we apply the bandages of money, schooling, food, etc., but if we leave people without Jesus—who is the only way to lasting hope, deliverance, and justice—are we ourselves acting justly?

> **Seeking justice without Jesus is like putting a bandage on a mortal wound.**

As we address injustice in the world, root issues must be tackled! Jesus said, "And you will know the truth, and the truth will set you free."[16] Will we live and proclaim truth instead of merely what is cool and acceptable in today's modern culture?

Jesus is essential for justice!

Join the Conversation

1. Why is understanding the true value of people so critical to bringing justice?

2. How is addressing justice without Jesus a bandage approach?

3. Why does Jesus often get left out of approaches to bring justice?

4

WITHHOLDING JESUS IS UNJUST

What kind of Christ-follower does not share Jesus?

I magine if there were a simple medicine available that could quickly cure any form of cancer. Now imagine what would happen if the owners of the drug's patent and formula decided to keep the drug a secret and only distribute the miracle drug to a few friends or people known to them. Only those who know the owners or who are in their good graces would know about and have access to this life-saving drug.

Such drug owners would be considered selfish, racist jerks by anyone who came to know about their actions. Why? Because the suffering and deaths of countless people could be stopped. The custodians of the medicine could make a huge difference, but instead, they selfishly choose not to do so. The drug owners' actions would be extraordinarily heartless and even unjust.

A sickness much worse than cancer has ravaged humanity. It has brought not only cancer but all kinds of sickness, poverty, hatred, and societal ills. Worst of all, this sickness has alienated human beings from their Creator and kept them from their true purpose in life. All of us have sinned and fallen short of the glory God has for us.[17] Sin and its source, satan, have caused immense injustice in this world.

As believers, we know the answer to this sickness. Jesus came as the Lamb of God to take away the sins of the world.[18] He came so that through His obedience, many would be made righteous.[19] He came that we would no longer be slaves to sin.[20]

Unfortunately, the "medicine" for injustice is still unknown and, thus, unavailable to over three billion people around the world. Nearly seven thousand people groups have no idea that Jesus came two thousand years ago to set them free. Two billion plus people have never heard of Christ's first coming, let alone His imminent return.

> If sin and satan are the root issues behind the world's injustice, then keeping people from the antidote (Jesus) is presently the world's greatest injustice!

In many ways, the Church is like the miracle drug owner. If sin and satan are the root issues behind the world's injustice, then keeping people from the antidote (Jesus) is presently the world's greatest injustice! Today, millions upon millions of people have no hope for true justice because they have never had the opportunity to experience Him who is the way, the truth, and the life.

Shakeel is from a poor Muslim family in South Asia. For the past several years, he has been unable to work because of suffering from epilepsy. None of his family members had the patience to live with him, so they all abandoned him. Even though he is about forty years old, Shakeel came to us like an orphan in many ways.

Shakeel went to multiple doctors and shamans without receiving any relief from the seizures and pain. Then he came to our church asking for healing. Believers prayed for Shakeel, and for the first time in about six years, Shakeel did not feel pain in his neck. God touched Shakeel!

The day we prayed for Shakeel was the day he heard the gospel for the first time. The day he heard, Shakeel asked Christ into his heart. Shakeel began a journey that we believe will see his eternal destiny changed.

Shakeel has suffered many injustices, including poverty, abandonment, and unemployment. The worst of these injustices, though, is that Shakeel lived over forty years without having a chance to encounter Christ.

Shakeel lived forty years . . . without ever hearing the gospel.

Unfortunately, Shakeel's story is not unusual. He represents three billion people around the world who are still waiting to hear about the honest answer to the injustices they face. Will you be a part of helping them hear? Will you be a part of stopping this injustice?

Join the Conversation

1. Why do many believers keep Jesus to themselves?

2. How can not sharing Jesus with the unreached be considered the world's greatest injustice today?

3. What can we do to encourage the church to share Jesus?

5

JUSTICE MATTERS FOR THE UNREACHED

Is it fair that millions never hear about Jesus?

While waiting at a South Asian train station for my friend to pick me up, Raj, a hard-working rickshaw driver, kept offering to take me places. Twice I turned Raj down, assuring him that my friend was coming to pick me up so I did not need a ride. After Raj's third attempt to get me to employ him, I felt a nudge by the Holy Spirit to start a conversation with Raj about Christ.

"Have you ever heard of Jesus Christ?" I asked Raj.

Raj looked me straight in the eyes and said, "Yes! I will take you there now. . . " What Raj meant was, "I will take you to the Jesus Hotel or to the Jesus Restaurant."

Raj had no clue who Jesus was. His offer to "take me there" broke my heart. Raj thought Jesus was a *place,* maybe a hotel, a restaurant, or a store. As I began to share the gospel with Raj, I discovered he had never heard the name of Jesus before. Never.

Though Raj worked in a capital city with millions of people, a city filled with all kinds of media and technology, Raj's language, caste, and social standing had isolated him from the message of Christ. Raj had never heard the gospel—he had no idea how to have a relationship with his Creator, how to have his sins forgiven, and how to experience true peace.

Raj's story is tragic, and it is far too common. Though we in the West do not encounter many who are utterly ignorant of Jesus, millions in other areas of the world have never had a chance to hear the gospel. Of the 17,314 people groups in the world, 7,279 are still considered unreached. This means approximately 42% of the people groups in the world today have not had the opportunity to hear the gospel.[21]

Roughly three billion people on the planet have not heard even one time a presentation of the gospel of Jesus Christ. Think about it—as you are reading this paragraph, three billion people are living and breathing and going about their daily schedule without any idea that God came to earth and died on the cross for their salvation. That should bother us . . . a lot.

Joshua Project defines an *unreached people group* as "a people group among which there is no indigenous community of believing Christians with adequate numbers and resources to evangelize this people group." Initially, this meant that unreached people groups were made up of less than 2% Evangelical Christians and less than 5% Christian adherents.[22] While the percentages are somewhat arbitrary, the great need for the gospel to be planted in every people group is not.

The difference between a reached people group and an unreached one is simple. People in reached people groups can hear the gospel and experience Christ. While some in these reached people groups may choose not to respond to Christ, there is at least the *opportunity* to hear. There are people within their people group who can share about Christ.

People in unreached people groups have no opportunity to hear the gospel. Language, ethnicity, socio-economic status, religion, and location keep them isolated from Christ-followers. Todd Johnson notes that 86% of Muslims, Hindus, and

Buddhists do not know a Christian.[23] They have no one in their circle of relationships who can share the love of Christ with them. These unreached are not just lost; they are, in a sense, cluelessly lost—not realizing their spiritual deadness nor being aware of how Christ wants to remedy their situation. They are unfairly isolated from the hope of Christ, without any idea how to obtain salvation.

Jesus commissioned His church nearly two thousand years ago to make disciples of all nations (Greek *ethne*, from which we get "ethnic or people groups" in English). It is unfair that any people group should be unreached at this point in history. Every people group is valuable to God and deserves an opportunity to choose Christ. Jesus did His part—He gave His life for them. Now, it is time for us to do our part and give every person on the planet a chance to hear the gospel.

> It is unfair that any people group should be unreached at this point in history.

What will you do to bring justice to those who have never had an opportunity to know Christ?

Join the Conversation

1. Have you ever met anyone who had never heard of Jesus or the gospel? What was your experience like?

2. What is the difference between a lost person in a reached people group and a lost person in an unreached people group?

3. What would living your whole life without hearing the gospel be like? Imagine how your mindset, emotions, and daily life would be affected.

6

BLAMING GOD

Whose fault is it that so many still have not heard?

J esus paid the highest price possible for humans to have a relationship with Him. He left the grandeur of heaven to be born in a stable. He lived as an ordinary Israelite and then chose to sacrifice His life in the most humiliating and painful death Romans knew how to inflict. Jesus went through all this so that whosoever believes in Him would not perish but have eternal life.[24]

Yet, despite the great love and sacrifice Jesus exhibited, many blame God for the injustice of the unreached. Many have questioned God's goodness and justice by asking,

"If God really cares about all people, why have some not heard?"

"Does God not care about people in remote places?"

"If God really cares about all people, then why doesn't He proclaim the gospel over megaphones to everyone?"

"Why doesn't God sovereignly make a way for all to have access to Him?"

It's difficult to understand all of God's ways fully. His ways are higher than ours, and His plans are beyond our comprehension.[25]

Yet, we cannot question God's heart for all nations. Jesus paid the ultimate price—His life—so that every unreached people group would have an opportunity to experience the life that only He can give. Jesus' sacrifice emphasizes His heart for all nations.

Though we as humans often want to blame God or others, we also cannot question the responsibility God gave us, His church. In His last words, Jesus highlighted His heart and said that not one person should be unreached—Jesus commanded His followers to go into all the world and make disciples of every nation.

The Great Commission is explicit in each of the Gospels and Acts:

+ And Jesus came and said to them, "All authority in heaven and on earth has been given to me. Go therefore and make disciples of all nations, baptizing them in the name of the Father and of the Son and of the Holy Spirit, teaching them to observe all that I have commanded you. And behold, I am with you always, to the end of the age." (Matthew 28:18–20)

+ And he said to them, "Go into all the world and proclaim the gospel to the whole creation. Whoever believes and is baptized will be saved, but whoever does not believe will be condemned. And these signs will accompany those who believe: in my name, they will cast out demons; they will speak in new tongues; they will pick up serpents with their hands; and if they drink any deadly poison, it will not hurt them; they will lay their hands on the sick, and they will recover." (Mark 16:15–18)

+ Then he opened their minds to understand the Scriptures, and said to them, "Thus it is written, that the

Christ should suffer and on the third day rise from the
dead, and that repentance for the forgiveness of sins
should be proclaimed in his name to all nations, begin-
ning from Jerusalem. You are witnesses of these things."
(Luke 24:45–48)

◆ Jesus said to them again, "Peace be with you. As the
Father has sent me, even so I am sending you." And
when he had said this, he breathed on them and said to
them, "Receive the Holy Spirit. If you forgive the sins of
any, they are forgiven them; if you withhold forgiveness
from any, it is withheld." (John 20:21–23)

◆ But you will receive power when the Holy Spirit has
come upon you, and you will be my witnesses in Jerusalem and in all Judea and Samaria, and to the end of the
earth. (Acts 1:8)

Christ's commission is clear, yet the enemy has deceived
many in the church into not taking responsibility for making
disciples of all nations. One way this has occurred is through a
twisted view of God's sovereignty. An overemphasis on God's
sovereignty kept many before William Carey from going to
the nations. The prevailing belief in Carey's day was that God
would sovereignly cause the gospel to go forth in His way.

William Carey valued God's sovereignty but recognized
the need to take action. On May 31, 1792, Carey addressed
fellow Baptist ministers and proposed a then-radical idea:
sending missionaries from England to India. As he spoke, an
older pastor rebuked Carey, expressing the mentality of that
day: "Young man, sit down: when God pleases to convert the
heathen, he will do it without your aid or mine."[26]

Sadly, even today, some equate God's sovereignty and
divine will with whatever happens in life. God is sovereign,

but not everything that happens is His will. God has clearly stated that it is not His will that any should perish,[27] yet many do. God has said that He wants all to be saved and come to a knowledge of the truth,[28] yet many have not come to a knowledge of the truth. Jesus commanded His church on multiple occasions to share the gospel, making it clear that God expects His church to participate in seeing His will be done. Blaming God for the world's unreached is foolish when we, His church, have not heeded His command to go and make disciples.

> Jesus paid the highest price possible for humans to have a relationship with Him.

Carey understood God intended people to play a role in taking the gospel to unreached places and He gave His life to reach the people of India. Since Carey, many believers have grasped the importance of obedience to Christ's commands and have spread the good news around the world. Many nations, however, still do not have access. Rather than blaming God for our undone work, we must focus on the task Christ has given us of taking the gospel to all nations.

Join the Conversation

1. How has Christ proven His concern for the unreached of the world?

2. Which version of the Great Commission stands out the most to you? Why?

3. Historically, a wrong view of God's sovereignty has kept many believers from pursuing the Great Commission. What other wrong beliefs keep the church from proclaiming the gospel to all nations?

7

INJUSTICE AT THE HANDS OF THE CHURCH

What does the church offer that no one else can?

Government and charitable organizations are engaging social justice issues across the planet: The BBC and CNN are fighting trafficking, the United Nations is fighting illiteracy and poverty, and the Red Cross is fighting AIDS. Even Hollywood has joined the effort. Seeing the networking and collaboration among individuals and organizations as they work to see justice given is tremendous. As believers, we should rejoice whenever people care about the needs of others. God is love, and He even uses people who do not know Him to alleviate temporal suffering.

As the church, however, we have a *unique role in society* and we must take it seriously. Jesus told His disciples to disciple all nations. We, the church, are Christ's ambassadors to a world that desperately needs to be reconciled to Him.[29] News stations are not qualified to fulfill that role. Governments are not signing up people to share Jesus with the unreached. Charities (even many Christian charities) are not sharing the gospel with people groups who have never heard.

Only the church can represent Christ to a world that is dying without Him. Only the church can finish the task Christ gave us. Only the church is responsible for stopping the injustice of being unreached with the gospel.

Today's church has extraordinary technology, unprecedented travel ability, and immense financial resources. Yet, billions of people remain in environments without access to the gospel. How can the church sit back and continue to permit such injustice?

This is not fair! The church's allowing 7,279 people groups to be unreached is not just! Yes, it is wrong for someone to be enslaved in poverty, to suffer with AIDS, or to go without clean water, but it is even more wrong for believers to allow billions to live and die without ever having a chance to follow Christ.

Christ-followers must wake up. We must cry out for those who have never had an opportunity to know **Jesus**, the ultimate answer to every justice issue. We point fingers at pimps for the way they use women. We point fingers at governments that misuse funds and abuse the poor. We need to point fingers at ourselves! We have been disobedient to Christ's command. We have not valued what He values. With the wealth and technology we have available, we should have completed Christ's final command long ago, and yet we still have 7,279 groups of people with no access to the gospel. That is three billion people too many!

> Only the church is responsible for stopping the injustice of being unreached with the gospel.

The Bread of Life is needed in every hungry child's home. Jehovah Jireh, God our Provider, is essential in every struggling economy. Unreached nations oppressed by pornography and prostitution need to encounter a holy and loving God who fully understands their worth and wants to set them free. Members of every unreached people group need to experience the purpose for which their Creator fashioned them. The unreached must be given the opportunity to know Jesus.

Join the Conversation

1. What should our attitude be toward secular organizations that address injustice?

2. What is our unique role as the church, and why is it so important?

3. How has the church de-emphasized Christ in its pursuit of seeking justice?

8
___

THE WORLD'S WORST INJUSTICE: REMEMBERED & REPLAYED

What is the worst injustice that has ever occurred?

The World's Worst Injustice Remembered

T he worst injustice the world has ever witnessed occurred about two thousand years ago when Jesus Christ was crucified. Merriam-Webster's dictionary defines injustice as either the absence of justice or the violation of the rights of another.[30] Christ's crucifixion fits both definitions. Justice has never been more absent than when Jesus was crucified. No one's rights have been violated more than Jesus' rights.

Justice was *totally* absent during Christ's crucifixion because Jesus was *totally innocent*. He was more innocent than any person has ever been. Besides Him, no one has ever lived who has not committed at least one sin.[31] Jesus, however, never sinned.[32] Jesus challenged the Jews to find legitimate fault with Him, and they could not.[33] Jesus had absolutely nothing in His life to merit punishment.

> The worst injustice the world has ever witnessed occurred about two thousand years ago when Jesus Christ was crucified.

Illegal Aspects of Jesus' Trial

The massive violation of Jesus' rights further emphasizes the incomparable injustice Jesus faced. Flagrant abuses of ecclesiastical power during the trial process violated Jewish protocol. Laws were broken left and right. The wrongs committed against Christ during His trials include:[34]

1. The time of day for the trial was unlawful. Part of Jesus' trial took place at night,[35] which was illegal for capital offense charges in their culture. Additionally, the Sanhedrin was not supposed to try cases until after the morning sacrifice.

2. A sole judge questioned Jesus in the trial (either Annas or Caiaphas in John 18:19). Law required more than one judge to be involved in the trial process.

3. The specific day of Jesus' trial was illegal because the trial was held on a feast day, which Jewish law forbade. Jesus enjoyed the Passover with His disciples on the first day of the Feast of Unleavened Bread. That very night, Jesus was arrested, and the next day, Friday, He was crucified.[36]

4. The speed of the trial was illegal. A capital case was concluded in less than twenty-four hours. The law required at least a day between the trial and the judgment decree. Jesus, however, was tried, condemned, and killed in far less than twenty-four hours.

5. The location (Caiaphas' house) where the Sanhedrin gave the death decree was illegal.[37] According to Jewish law at that time, the temple was the only location acceptable for capital decrees.

6. The prejudice against Jesus expressed by members of the Sanhedrin legally disqualified them from pronouncing a decree of death on Jesus.

7. The corruption within the high priesthood further testifies to the inequity of Jesus' trial. Josephus and others have testified that the high priesthood was often given to the highest bidder.

8. Injustice continued as false witnesses testified against Jesus.[38] When witnesses lie, justice is perverted.

9. Jesus' trial was illegal because no one called for witnesses to testify on Jesus' behalf.

10. Pilate could name no wrong Jesus had done, nor could the crowd when Pilate asked them. Yet, in the end, for political expediency, Pilate handed Jesus over for death.[39]

Extreme Shame and Extreme Pain

Not only did Jesus' trials demonstrate extreme injustice, so also did the punishment he received: crucifixion. Crucifixion signified extreme shame. It was deemed the most disgraceful punishment the Romans practiced. Only slaves, the basest of criminals, and offenders who were not Roman citizens could be executed on crosses. The person being crucified was stripped of his clothes and hung in a public place to be mocked and ridiculed by all who passed.

Crucifixion also meant extreme pain. Romans were experts at inflicting pain on their enemies and fear in the hearts of those who might go against Rome's wishes. Crucifixion was a tool in their arsenal of intimidation to keep would-be rebels in submission. Professional torturers killed Jesus.

Two nails were driven through Jesus' wrists. Another nail was driven through His ankles. These three nails are what physically held His body on the cross. Jesus was forced to pull against the pieces of iron in His wrists as He gasped for air by pushing down on the nail that crushed His feet together. Each push and each pull sent searing pain throughout the nerves in His body. It is not possible to overestimate the amount of pain Jesus endured for us on the cross.

And let's not forget all the pain He endured before the cross. He was hit and punched. His beard was pulled out, and a crown of thorns was pushed into His skull. A whip with pieces of glass, bone, and metal attached was raked over His body thirty-nine times. Talk about inhumane treatment! Jesus' body was beaten beyond recognition before He ever got to the cross.

Emotional Agony

In addition to the immense physical pain suffered by Jesus during the crucifixion and the hours beforehand, He also experienced intense emotional agony. We see a glimpse of Jesus' agony as He prayed in the garden of Gethsemane just before His arrest. His capillaries burst from stress, and He sweats blood.[40] Jesus had grown up seeing men hang on crosses. He knew the great challenge of the cross, but He was also aware of how much depended on His enduring the cross.[41] He who knew no sin was made to be sin that we might be made the righteousness of God in Him.[42]

Becoming sin for us, Jesus endured the emotional agony of being separated from God the Father. "My God, my God, why have you forsaken me?"[43] He uttered as He experienced suffering and pain beyond comprehension. Though Jesus had done nothing worthy of such a punishment, Jesus allowed Himself to experience the agony of being denied access to God's presence. Jesus, Love Himself, laid His life down in the presence of hatred.

The World's Worst Injustice Replayed

Sadly, the injustice Christ experienced is perpetuated over and over today. Millions upon millions for whom Christ paid the ultimate price have never heard of His love. They have no idea He faced injustice so that the causes of their injustice could be addressed.

Some time back, a Nepali man worked with our family, and I had daily opportunities to talk with him about Christ. During the first of these conversations, I was shocked to hear that he had never heard of Jesus before. Though he was twenty-seven years old and living in one of the world's largest metropolitan areas—not in any way geographically isolated— Ramu had never heard the gospel, and Ramu did not have any idea who Jesus was. As my family shared with Ramu, God worked in Ramu's heart, and today, he is serving Christ with his whole family!

Allowing history's worst injustice to go unknown is the most significant form of injustice we allow in today's world. It is wrong not to share the good news of Christ's work on the cross. It is wrong to ignore people groups for whom Jesus paid the ultimate price, His life.

The church, God's people, must stop this injustice from raging onward. Every group of people alive today deserves an opportunity to know about the injustice Christ suffered for them. They have the right to choose whether to follow Him or not. They deserve a chance to hear.

Join the Conversation

1. What part of the injustice Christ faced during the time of His crucifixion impacts you the most emotionally?

2. What were some of the wrongs Christ faced in His trial?

3. What can you do to keep Christ's injustice from continually being replayed?

9

GOSPEL PRIVILEGE

What is our response to the privilege of knowing Christ?

In 2 Kings chapter 7, four Israeli men with leprosy were starving at the city gate in Samaria. In desperation, they decided to surrender to their enemies, the Syrians, hoping for mercy. At dusk, they went toward the Syrians' camp.

No one was there when they reached the edge of the Syrians' camp. God had caused the Syrians to hear the sound of chariots, horses, and a great army, so all the Syrians fled and left almost everything behind.

The four men entered one of the tents and ate to their hearts' content before taking gold, silver, and clothes. After hiding these treasures, they went into another tent and took more things. They then hid those treasures and said to each other, "We are not doing right. This is a day of good news. If we are silent and wait until morning light, punishment will overtake us. Now therefore come; let us go and tell the king's household."

So the four went and called out to the city gatekeepers of Samaria and told them what they had experienced. The king sent a search party to verify the truth of the story. After the search party verified the truth of the Syrians' flight, the people of Samaria went out and plundered the Syrians' camp. The treasure found by four Israeli lepers was shared with the city of Samaria.

This story, however, could have gone in a different direction. The four lepers had likely been among the least privileged people in Samaria. They were forced to live outside the city gate because of their illness. They were outcasts, isolated from the rest of society as they longed for food. Finding the Syrians' treasure suddenly afforded the four immense privileges, options for a new life, and possibly a means of revenge on those who had excluded them. The four lepers could have established a settlement where lepers ruled and where they had special status. They could have forgotten about the many starving people in Samaria. After all, their needs were met.

> We, like the four Israelis with leprosy, are privileged with good news, and we must grasp our responsibility to share this privilege with others.

The four soon recognized that their newfound privilege of wealth and knowledge was not just to elevate their financial status and give them a better life. They felt a sense of responsibility to pass on the blessing God had provided for them. They chose to share the news of the abandoned Syrians' camp. Samaria was immensely blessed as a result.

As followers of Christ, we are privileged with the gospel! We have good news that we have heard and experienced, yet so many in our world have not experienced the blessings of the gospel, which changes lives on earth and for eternity. We, like the four Israelis with leprosy, are privileged with good news, and we must grasp our responsibility to share this privilege with others.

David Joannes, in his book, *Gospel Privilege: The Unearned Advantage that's Meant for Everyone*, notes that the phrase "gospel privilege" first appeared in 1658 on the third page of Puritan preacher Isaac Ambrose's work, *Looking Unto Jesus:*

> I shall make this my design to look at Jesus more especially, as carrying on the great work of our salvation from first to last. This, indeed, is the glad tidings, the gospel, the gospel-privilege, and our gospel-duty: 'Looking unto Jesus.'[44]

In the early 1700s, Matthew Henry also wrote about gospel privilege, often emphasizing that Christians' privilege requires a response:

> What is our great gospel privilege—that God has called us to his kingdom and glory. . . . What is our great gospel duty—that we walk worthy of God, that the temper of our minds and tenour of our lives be answerable to this call and suitable to this privilege. We should accommodate ourselves to the intention and design of the gospel and live suitably to our profession and privileges, our hopes and expectations, as becomes those who are called with such a high and holy calling.[45]

Joannes further writes that nineteenth-century Christians were informed by the concept that the gospel brought privilege, and privilege included responsibility. According to a search on Google Ngram Viewer, this concept came to be used colloquially between 1810 and 1888.[46]

Today, Christians are more likely to refer to themselves as blessed by God than as privileged. However, Christians are both: God has blessed us, and God has privileged us. In both cases, we, as Christians, are responsible for sharing what Christ has done for us.

Just as the four Israeli lepers recognized they needed to share the news of their fortune, we as believers must let others know how they, too, can have the privileged status of being reconciled to God.

Join the Conversation

1. How would you have reacted if you were one of the lepers in Israel who found the deserted camp?

2. How should gospel privilege lead to a sense of responsibility?

3. What are some examples of gospel privilege in your life?

10

GOSPEL INEQUALITY

How concerned are we about gospel access?

Economic inequality surrounds the globe. A relatively small percentage of people own a high percentage of the world's resources. Certain national economies are also far more robust than other national economies. The average person in North America or Western and Northern Europe is far wealthier than the average person in other developing areas. Even within families with the same parents, some siblings are often more affluent than others.

While Christians should be concerned about economics and stewardship, gospel inequality has a much graver eternal impact than economic inequality. Gospel access is far from equal. About thirty percent of the world identifies as "Christian" and has access to Christ's good news. Roughly another thirty percent of the world lives next to those claiming to be Christians, sharing their cultures, languages, castes, incomes, and ethnicities. This second group also has access to the gospel as the Christians among them share the good news.

Yet another 42% of the world cannot access the gospel. They are considered unreached, still living isolated from the gospel and Christians who can share Christ with them. This 42% of the world exemplifies gospel inequality, representing the worst example of inequality in the world. It has been over two thousand years since Christ gave us the Great Commission, yet so many still live isolated from the good news!

Jesus' concern regarding gospel inequality stands out in Mark 11 when He entered the temple courts in Jerusalem. Jesus began overturning the money changers' tables. John's account shares Jesus even used a whip.[47] Scripture rarely depicts Jesus as angry, yet Jesus is clearly angry in this passage.

Jesus' anger was not focused on currency exchange or business activity though. Jesus was disturbed about access to God. The Court of the Gentile, where the merchandise was being sold, was the only location in the temple where non-Jewish people could connect with God. The atmosphere of the one place where the Gentiles could experience God had been ruined by people more interested in making money than making things right with their Creator. Jesus, passionate for all ethnicities to access the table of God's kingdom, quoted Isaiah 56:7, "My house shall be called a house of prayer for all peoples."[48] Jesus was disturbed that the Jews, who had so much access to God, were not concerned about the Gentiles, who had so little.

Just as where you live on earth determines whether you have access to clean water, education, and economic opportunity, where you live often also determines whether or not you have access to the gospel. This reality affects over three billion people today—over three billion people who are unreached and gospel deprived: Deprived of the good news . . . deprived of Jesus . . . deprived of hope . . . deprived of true life. This inequality should not be the case two thousand years after Christ. How concerned are we about people having access to the gospel?

Further adding to gospel inequality is realizing that the countries with the most Christians often receive the largest numbers of missionaries. There are many reasons for this, but one stems from the locations of most short-term missions trips. Most short-term trips result from invitations from churches in other countries who are able to host teams. Christians in one host country frequently invite Christians from other countries to serve them via missions work in their country.[49] This reliance on invitations from other Christians for trips can lead to an imbalance in missionary sending, as many missionaries sense God calling them to serve in the first country they experience on a cross-cultural trip. Countries able to invite and host other Christians tend to receive many more missionaries than other countries who do not have churches to invite missionaries. One dramatic example is the comparison of Brazil (a majority Christian country), which receives twenty thousand missionaries, with Bangladesh (a majority Muslim country), with nearly as many people, which receives only a thousand missionaries.[50]

> Jesus was disturbed that the Jews, who had so much access to God, were not concerned about the Gentiles, who had so little.

As Christ-followers, we must oppose gospel inequality and be concerned about sharing our privileges in Christ with the many who have unequal access to Christ's love. Jesus paid the price for all nations. May we be a part of them learning the price He paid!

Join the Conversation

1. Why do you think gospel inequality exists?

2. Why do locations or people groups with many Christians often receive many missionaries and short-term teams while countries with little access do not?

3. What is God asking you to do to address gospel inequality?

11

ROADBLOCKS TO JUSTICE

Why do the unreached remain unreached?

Why do so many nations remain unreached two thousand years after Christ commissioned His church to disciple all nations? In an age of massive travel and communication advancements, how can so many people still be ignorant of the good news? In this chapter, we will look at some of the causes of this sad reality.

Limited Access

Culture, religion, language, and geography isolate people groups. Unreached people groups often are part of cultures and religious systems that are incredibly resistant to influence from outside sources. Other unreached people groups are isolated by a mother tongue that is difficult for outsiders to learn. Still other people groups are unreached because of their geographic location. These groups are not conveniently situated near existing churches. They are not found in places that make for an easy life. It's not easy to reach out to any of the people groups who remain unreached. That is precisely why so many of these groups remain unreached. If it were easy, it would already be done.

Many believers point to the internet as the answer for taking the gospel to the unreached. Yes, the internet is a tool used to spread the gospel, but we cannot rely only on this tool. The internet is an excellent resource for sharing Jesus, but only about 66% of the world's population has internet access.[51] The situation is often worse in areas where the gospel has spread the least. For example, internet penetration is far less in rural Asia and Africa.[52] Poverty and government restrictions in least-reached areas further limit internet usage by those who most need to hear the good news.

In addition to the other factors we have discussed that limit access to the gospel, illiteracy further restricts access. Many of the world's unreached are illiterate and oral learners. Illiteracy often hinders people from exposure to new ideas, including the gospel. Oral learners process information differently, relying heavily on stories and music. Illiterates and oral learners have limited access to the gospel because most gospel presentations are printed or follow Western (outlined) thought processes.

Limited Giving to the Unreached

Only a tiny percentage of Christian income is invested in reaching the unreached. Only 0.1% of all Christian giving is directed toward mission efforts in the thirty-eight most unevangelized countries in the world.[53] Money alone is not what is needed to reach millions without Jesus, but money is a necessary tool. More can and should be done financially to prioritize the unreached. Resources must be utilized for training and sending frontier workers who will see God's kingdom established among unreached people groups.

De-emphasis on Apostolic Ministry

God used the apostolic ministry of Jesus to bring the kingdom of heaven to the world. He used Jesus' disciples and Paul as apostles to spread the good news and start believing communities in many different cultures. In the West today, outside of some Charismatic and African-American circles, very few traditions acknowledge the role of apostles (and in some charismatic environments the word *apostle* is seemingly misused as another word for "super pastor" or the head of the organization). Pastors, teachers, and evangelists are widely appreciated in the body of Christ, but apostles (and prophets) often do not get recognized.[54] The vital ministry of apostles must be encouraged so that the church expands into new areas. *Apostle* comes from the Greek *apostello,* "to send."

> The gospel is only good news if it gets there in time.
> —Carl F. H. Henry[60]

Apostles are by nature "sent ones," and many are needed today to lay the foundations for the kingdom among new people groups.[55] They, like Paul, are not content to build on others' foundations. They want to see Jesus glorified among new *ethne!*[56]

Lack of Emphasis on God's Power

While most Christians in the majority of the world acknowledge the spiritual world and understand the importance of spiritual power, many Westerners do not. Westerners must emphasize God's power in their outreach to be effective in unreached contexts. Jesus promised His disciples power from the Holy Spirit to be witnesses for Him. That power is needed not only by apostles but also by all believers to share Christ in pioneer environments.

Very few Muslims, Hindus, or Buddhists decide to follow Christ without experiencing some supernatural event. The power of God is essential to open the hearts and minds of people groups who live in a different paradigm of life. Logic and well-thought-out sermons usually are not enough to convince Muslims, Hindus, or Buddhists to follow Christ. The unreached must experience God's power!

Limited Concern for Eternal Suffering

As secularism and materialism have de-emphasized the reality of the supernatural, many Christians have focused more on physical suffering. Eternity and eternal suffering have been minimized as many in the church have been discipled in secularism. This de-emphasis on eternity leads many in the West to emphasize social action—fixing problems we can see with our physical eyes and tangibly experience. As we have stated throughout this book, all suffering matters to God. Believers should demonstrate love in tangible ways, but eternal suffering is also real and must truly grab our hearts. The reality of hell must become real again to God's people. People live forever in one of two places. The church must regain a passion for delivering people groups from eternal suffering.

Spiritual Warfare

Contrary to the claims of secular humanism and materialism, a real spiritual battle exists in the world today. Many people groups are still unreached because the enemy of their souls wants to keep the gospel away from them. The enemy does not want to give up territory. Spiritual warfare is real. The enemy has enjoyed centuries of domination over many unreached people groups and does not surrender easily. Paul told the Ephesian church: "For we do not wrestle against flesh and blood, but against the rulers, against the authorities, against the cosmic powers over this present darkness, against the spiritual forces of evil in the heavenly places."[57]

Christ-followers reaching the unreached must entirely depend on the Holy Spirit's power. Spiritual ground is not gained through mere human effort or strength. As Zechariah wrote many years ago, "'Not by might, nor by power, but by my Spirit,' says the LORD of hosts."[58] Only through God's power can we make progress in discipling the nations.

D-I-S-O-B-E-D-I-E-N-C-E

Disobedience on the part of Christ's church is the primary reason unreached people groups still exist two thousand years after Christ commissioned us to disciple all nations.

Much of the early church stayed in Jerusalem until persecution forced them to move and share the good news in other locations.[59] However, Christ's body has often shirked its responsibility to bring Jesus to the nations. It is much easier to stay in our familiar Jerusalems than to spread out to the unreached.

Discipling all nations takes work. There are many obstacles. Some of these are evident from a distance, but many are not. Stepping out in obedience is a prerequisite for God's ever-unfolding revelation of how to reach the unreached and disciple nations. God does not reveal His strategies and ways to arm-chair or ivory-tower pew-sitters. He blesses those who use the talents they have. He gives insight to those who attempt obedience so that they can know the steps and means necessary to complete His vision.

As we have shared earlier, in all four of the Gospel accounts and Acts, Jesus emphasized the church is sent to the nations in His last words:

- Go therefore and make disciples of all nations. (Matthew 28:19)

- Go into all the world and proclaim the gospel to the whole creation. (Mark 16:15)

- Repentance for the forgiveness of sins should be proclaimed in his name to all nations. (Luke 24:47)

- As the Father has sent me, even so I am sending you. (John 20:21)

- But you will receive power when the Holy Spirit has come upon you; and you will be my witnesses in Jerusalem and in all Judea and Samaria, and to the end of the earth. (Acts 1:8)

Jesus' last words are significant. He wanted to emphasize His heart for all people and our role in helping all people access Him. Jesus expects His church to step out in obedience to His last command. He paid the price for all nations to know Him. We must obey Jesus and finish the task He has given us to do.

Join the Conversation

1. Which roadblocks bother you the most?

2. Do you agree that disobedience is the most significant roadblock? Why or why not?

3. What is one thing you can do to address a roadblock given in this chapter?

12

WHAT CAN I DO?

What can one person do to make a difference?

Several years back, my wife and I lived in the mountains of Southern Asia. While we were eating dinner, we heard a commotion outside. Walking out the door, we saw a terrified little girl being chased by her mother. The mother was in a rage because one of the flowers in her garden had been broken off—she was chasing her daughter with a large stick to beat her for what she had done. My wife grabbed the little girl and told the mother, in effect, "You will touch this little girl with that stick over my dead body." My wife was outraged at how this little girl was being treated, and my wife was willing to take a hit to keep the girl safe.

Our hearts are stirred when we hear of a child being physically or emotionally abused. Yet every day, millions upon millions of God's children are being abused by the tormentor of all tormentors. We cannot even begin to imagine the evil that emanates from the devil—there is not even the tiniest shred of kindness in him. He torments people with temptation, guilt, fear, condemnation, hopelessness, pain, disease, and all other kinds of evil.

People deserve to know there is a way out. They need to know they can experience hope and peace. Millions of people need to hear there is an answer: Jesus. But remember, 42% of the world's people groups are still classified as unreached. They have no one to tell them about Christ and what He has done for them.

Your life can impact their lives. Your life can impact their eternities. The choice is yours. Will you choose to get involved or look the other way?

Please consider the following possible ways to impact those unreached with the good news . . .

Pray and Research

Nothing is more strategic than prayer! Ask God what He would have you do to impact the unreached. The needs of the unreached are overwhelming, but God has specific works He has prepared for you to do (Ephesians 2:10). Ask God what part He wants you to play in giving the gospel to those without access.

1. **Learn more about the unreached** for prayer. Here are some sites to visit:

   - https://agwm.org/en/ontheway/
   - https://www.joshuaproject.net/
   - https://operationworld.org/
   - https://www.livedead.org/
   - https://pray1040.com
   - https://www.thetravelingteam.org/stats

WHAT CAN I DO?

2. **Consider downloading an app** from the following organizations and movements to use for prayer and learning:
   - AGWM
   - Change the Map
   - Live Dead
   - On the Way

3. **Take a missions course** such as Perspectives on the World Christian Movement or other missions course in your area.

4. **Adopt a people group.**
   - After learning more about the unreached, pray about adopting a people group for daily prayer. Invest yourself emotionally with this people group. Cry for them. Be the person who will stand in the gap for them.

5. **Weekly fasting and prayer.**
   - Start or join a prayer and fasting time one day each week. Give up food during your lunch hour to pray that God's Spirit will be poured out on all unreached people groups. Invite colleagues, students, and friends to join. Consider receiving weekly prayer points for Muslims from Global Initiative at https://www.reachingmuslimpeoples.com/get-involved.

6. **Start a prayer group** in your local church.
   - Not only can the group pray corporately for unreached people groups, but it can also work to raise awareness of unreached people groups.

7. Use Prayercast videos.

- ◆ These two- to three-minute videos each focus on a particular country or people group in the world. They can be shown in churches, small groups, or other gatherings. They help stimulate prayer at any event, large or small. Find them at https://prayercast.com.

Give Financially to Impact the Unreached

We demonstrate what we care about by investing our time and our treasure. What do our personal, family, business, or church budgets say about our concern for those unreached with the good news? Does our spending align with our values?

1. Before you give to missions, **tithe to your local church**. God is a giver and wants us to look like Him. Don't give to get; give to look like your heavenly Father who never tires of giving.

2. After tithing to your church, **consider giving another percentage of your income** to spread the gospel globally. Making it a set percentage helps you budget and be intentional about giving. Consider increasing your missions giving percentage every year.

3. **Participate in Faith Promise giving.** If your church collects regular missions monthly pledges, give faithfully and by faith. Believe the Lord to provide more than you are comfortable guaranteeing. Teach your children and other disciples to give. If your church does not collect mission pledges, look for missionaries you can support monthly.

4. **Assist missionaries** who are on itineration. When they are home from the field, loan them a car. Assist them with housing. Invest in missionary kids by caring for some needs not yet provided (e.g., a used car for college, a computer or tablet, sports equipment, etc.).

5. **Legacy giving.** Write unreached people groups into your will. Determine what percentage of your legacy giving you would like to be used to plant churches among unreached peoples and leverage your "home-going to glory" to help others find their way to their eternal home.

Go Locally and Globally

1. **Prayer walk.**

   ◆ Go to neighborhoods or areas where unreached populations live and pray for God to reveal Himself through dreams and visions. See whom God might lead you to talk or witness to.

2. **Reach out to people** where you are.

   ◆ Most colleges and universities have students from unreached people groups around the world. Immigrants from unreached people groups have settled in many places in the West. Start relationships where you are with those God has placed near you.

3. **Explore teaching English to immigrants** in your area.

   ◆ Teaching English is an excellent way to get to know people from unreached people groups and is a tool used around the world to open doors for sharing the gospel.

4. **Learn a language** that an unreached people group speaks.

> ◆ Many unreached people groups are isolated because of language. People willing to learn Arabic, Bengali, Dari, Gujarati, Hausa, Hindi, Japanese, Javanese, Thai, Turkish, Urdu, and other languages of the unreached are needed. Add a college class or find a language tutor in your city. We can only reach groups if we can communicate with them.

5. **Go and serve with a team** engaging the unreached.

> ◆ https://www.livedead.org/

> ◆ https://wideopenmissions.org/ (Share that you specifically want to serve with a church-planting team working with unreached people groups.)

Going to where the unreached are located will cost more than other trips. It will take more money and more time, but it will open your eyes to the vast need of entire societies who have yet to hear the gospel message one time.

Join the Conversation

1. What step could you take today to bring more justice to the unreached?

2. What goal would God have you set for your family's involvement?

3. What could you encourage your church to do to make a difference among the unreached?

.

NOTES

CHAPTER 1 ♦ THE SIGNIFICANCE OF JUSTICE

1. Matthew 22:39

CHAPTER 2 ♦ WHOLISTIC JUSTICE

2. Matthew 16:26

3. Luke 4:18–19 quoting Isaiah 61:1–2

4. John 4:24

5. 2 Corinthians 4:18

6. Spitters, Denny. *Conversations on When Everything Is Missions: Recovering the Mission of the Church*. BottomLine Media. Kindle Edition.

7. Mark 6:30-44; Mark 8:1-13

8. Leatherberry, David. *Pentecostalism and the Future of Missions* (Global Initiative, 2013), 20.

9. Matthew 16:26, emphasis added

CHAPTER 3 ♦ JESUS: ESSENTIAL FOR JUSTICE

10. Romans 3:23

11. Romans 6:22–23

12. John 10:10

13. 1 John 3:8

14. Luke 4:18

15. Matthew 22:39

16. John 8:32

CHAPTER 4 ♦ WITHHOLDING JESUS IS UNJUST

17. Romans 3:23

18. John 1:29

19. Romans 5:19

20. Romans 6:6

CHAPTER 5 ◆ JUSTICE MATTERS FOR THE UNREACHED

21. https://joshuaproject.net
22. https://joshuaproject.net/resources/articles/hijacking_unreached
23. https://lausanneworldpulse.com/research.php/856

CHAPTER 6 ◆ BLAMING GOD

24. John 3:16
25. Isaiah 55:9
26. https://www.christianity.com/church/church-history/time-line/1701-1800/william-carey-preached-deathless-sermon-11630317.html
27. 2 Peter 3:9
28. 1 Timothy 2:4

CHAPTER 7 ◆ INJUSTICE AT THE HANDS OF THE CHURCH

29. 2 Corinthians 5:20

CHAPTER 8 ◆ THE WORLD'S WORST INJUSTICE

30. https://www.merriam-webster.com/dictionary/injustice
31. Romans 3:23
32. Hebrews 4:15
33. John 8:46
34. Adapted from https://www.crosswalk.com/faith/bible-study/reasons-why-the-trial-of-jesus-was-illegal.html
35. Matthew 26:36–27:1
36. Leviticus 23:4–8, Matthew 26:17
37. Matthew 26:57–66
38. Mark 14:55–60
39. Matthew 27: 1–2, 11–26
40. Luke 22:44
41. Matthew 26:54
42. 2 Corinthians 5:21
43. Matthew 27:46

CHAPTER 9 ♦ GOSPEL PRIVILEGE

44. Joannes, David. *Gospel Privilege: The Unearned Advantage That's Meant for Everyone.* (Within Reach Global, 2021), Kindle Edition.

45. https://www.christianity.com/bible/commentary/Matthew-henry-complete/1-thessalonians/2#

46. https://books.google.com/ngrams/graph?corpus=26&-year_end=2019&content=Gospel+privilege&smoothing=3&year_start=1800&

CHAPTER 10 ♦ GOSPEL INEQUALITY

47. John 2:15

48. Mark 11:17, emphasis added

49. Johnson, Todd M., and Gina A. Zurlo. *World Christian Encyclopedia, 3rd Edition.* (Edinburgh University Press, 2019), 33.

50. Ibid.

CHAPTER 11 ♦ ROADBLOCKS TO JUSTICE

51. https://www.forbes.com/home-improvement/internet/internet-statistics/#:~:text=There%20are%205.35%20billion%20internet%20users%20worldwide.&text=Out%20of%20the%20nearly%208,the%20internet%2C%20according%20to%20Statista

52. https://joshuaproject.net/resources/articles/has_everyone_heard

53. Barrett, David B., and Todd M. Johnson. *World Christian Trends AD 30 - AD 2200: Interpreting the annual Christian Megacensus.* Associate ed. Christopher R. Guidry and Peter F. Crossing. (William Carey Library, 2001), 656.

54. Pastoral ministry is far more prevalent and recognized in the world today. Pastors are vitally needed for the care and equipping of local church bodies. Apostles are also desperately needed, though, to initiate new movements to Christ among the unreached.

55. Ephesians 2:20

56. Romans 15:20

57. Ephesians 6:12

58. Zechariah 4:6

59. Acts 8:1

60. Joannes, David. *Gospel Privilege: The Unearned Advantage That's Meant for Everyone.* (Within Reach Global, 2021), Kindle Edition.

www.ingramcontent.com/pod-product-compliance
Lightning Source LLC
Chambersburg PA
CBHW060417050426
42449CB00009B/2000